The Story of John the Baptist
Luke 1:5–80, Mark 1:1–8 for children

Written by Erik Rottmann
Illustrated by Michelle Dorenkamp

Arch® Books
Copyright © 2007 Concordia Publishing House
3558 S. Jefferson Avenue, St. Louis, MO 63118-3968
1-800-325-3040 • www.cph.org

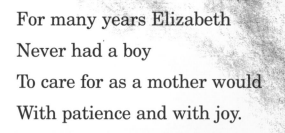

For many years Elizabeth
Never had a boy
To care for as a mother would
With patience and with joy.

But then one day an angel came
While Zechariah prayed.
He said, "Elizabeth shall bear
A son who will be great.

"Your boy will go before the Lord
To straighten out His way;
To break the stony hearts of men
And turn them into clay."

The aging Zechariah asked,
"How can this ever be?
Elizabeth is very old.
I'm not sure I believe!"

Because of this, the angel said,
"Your silence shall remain
Until the day your son is born
And you give him a name."

While John was in his mother's womb,
She heard a happy voice.
The mother of our Lord had come
To visit and rejoice!

As soon as Mary spoke her word
Of greeting, full of cheer,
John leapt for joy within the womb!
The Lamb of God was near!

The Virgin Mary also had
A baby on the way.
The Son of God had come to earth
To teach, to heal, to pray.

But more than that! Our Lord had come
To die upon a cross;
To take away the sin and death
That clings to each of us.

At last Elizabeth gave birth.
Her neighbors all were glad.
They thought her baby should receive
The name his father had.

Elizabeth said, "Not at all!
The baby's name is John."
Then Zechariah waved his hands
For something to write on.

With letters forming clear and bold,
"His name is John," he wrote.
Then God put Zechariah's voice
Back into his throat!

John's father sang with voice restored
A song of thanks and praise:
"God enables us to live
And serve Him all our days.

"And you, my child, shall go before
The Lamb who takes all sin.
You'll speak forgiveness, life, and light
By pointing us to Him."

John teaches us that children are
Sweet gifts from God above.
He gives them to their moms and dads
To cherish, hold, and love.

John also shows how God's strong Word
Gives faith to infant babes,
And small believers have a place
Among those whom He saves!

Dear Parents

"He will bless … both the small and the great" (Psalm 115:13). The story of John the Baptist's birth (Luke 1) provides a wonderful opportunity to teach your child about the gifts that God gives. First, John illustrates that there are no "accidental" births, but "children are a heritage from the LORD" (Psalm 127:3). After reading this story together, you could explain to your child that, just as God gave John to Zechariah and Elizabeth, so He also has given your child to you as a special blessing.

You could also use this story to teach your child that God gives the miraculous gift of faith (Ephesians 2:8, Romans 12:3) also to babies. When Jesus spoke about "these little ones who believe in Me" (Matthew 18:6), He included the smallest people of all: infants. Mary's voice proclaimed the nearness of the Christ, still in her womb. At the hearing of this Word, John leapt for joy in his mother's womb. Likewise, every child can hear the powerful, life-giving Word of God "from infancy" (2 Timothy 3:15, NIV). This hearing of the Word, rooted in Baptism, will result in eternal life for you and your child.

The Author